Daddy's Delici

First published in 2021

ISBN 978-1-8384639-0-8

"Oh I love the smell, I can smell it with my nose."
"I can see daddy cooking, I just can't stop looking."

"I can hear daddy
singing in the kitchen
he has a lovely melody."

I guess dinner is soon done.
I will share with you if you
want some.

I wash my hands and sit down around the table.

I am excited, I can't keep stable.
It's Sunday, it's Jamaica's best!

Rice and peas with brown stew chicken.

My vegetable
dish on the side.

I am not going out
even if my friends
invite me for a ride.

Yum! yum!
I thought to myself.

I heard the door open.

Daddy brings my dinner to me
as I said, "Thank you Daddy!"
He says, "you're welcome son."

Mum reminded me to say thank you to God. I did and took my knife and fork up.

My hands to feel...

as I took my chicken leg
in my hand.

The juice runs down my hand...

but mostly in my mouth.

My tongue was tasting
delicious flavours.

The rice and peas is
so shelly and nice.

I have to eat
all the peas and rice.

Mum said, "Eat up your veg."
I wasn't too happy but
I ate it though.

There was mashed potatoes
but I couldn't go no more.

My belly is full as I drank carrot juice..

Glug
Glug
My pants button
I had to loose.

I made a big belch,
and I said pardon me.

Daddy's delicious dinner
is the best.
After eating all this
I need to digest.
I am tired
but later I can rest.

Here are ten questions you can ask children about the story

1. What was the title of the story?

2. What was your favourite part of the story?

3. If you could change one thing in the story what would it be?

4. What was daddy's delicious dinner?

5.Can you name the senses they used in the story?

6. What did the boys do before they had their dinner?

7. Use a sentence to describe the dad in the story. Example: The dad enjoys cooking.

8. Who cooks the best in your family?

9. What did you like about this book?

10. Can you name 5 vegetables that appear in the book?

Spot the 6 differences!

S

Answers

1. Daddy's Delicious Dinner

2. My favourite part of the story was ______________________________________

3. If I could change one thing in the story, it would be ________________________

4. Daddy's Delicious Dinner was rice and peas

with brown stew chicken and a vegetable dish on the side.

5. They used all five senses:

Nose to smell, eyes to see, ears to listen,

hands to feel and touch, tongue to taste.

6. They washed their hands.

* It is vital to wash your hands for at least 20 seconds to help minimise the risk of spreading germs. Use soap and water and follow the right technique.

7.The dad in the story is___________________________________

8. ____________________ cooks the best in my family.

9. I like____best about the book.

10. There were red kidney beans, tomatoes,carrots, lettuce, aubergine, broccoli, courgette, and mashed potatoes !

*Tomatoes are referred to as vegetables by nutritionists, however tomatoes are fruits that have a ripened flower ovary and consist of seeds. It can be cooked or eaten raw. It has vitamin C and is very good for the skin and body.

Spot the difference: Pocket on jumping boy, salt shaker by stove, one music note missing, table cloth is set differently, there's a fork and knife on the table, only one sunflower..

Colour in the picture yourself!

Colour in the picture yourself

Recipe for Daddy's Delicious Dinner!

Brown stew chicken ingredients.

- Chopped whole or boneless chicken.
- 1 whole diced onion
- 2 ripe tomatoes chopped
- 4 tsp all purpose seasoning
- 2 fresh thymes
- 1 scallions
- 1/2 tsp paprika
- 2tsp salt
- 1/2 tsp ground black pepper
- 2 carrots sliced
- 5tsp spoon sunflower oil
- 1/2 cup ketchup
- 2 cups of water

Instructions

- Wash chicken with lemon and water or you can use vinegar and water. Remove all skin and cut into small pieces.

- In a large bowl ,combine onions, scallions, garlic, thyme, paprika, 2 tsp teaspoon salt and ½ teaspoon black pepper. Add the chicken and massage the marinade into the chicken, rub well for even coat. Cover the bowl and allow to marinate for some hours or even overnight.

- Heat the oil in a large heavy-bottomed pot until hot, about 5 minutes.Add the chicken to the hot oil and fry, turning it occasionally, until deep brown on all sides, about 10 minutes total.

- Once all chicken pieces are brown, place all the cutted vegetables in another pot, use some of the oil from the pot the chicken was fried in to add in another pot.Add 2 cups of water,1/2 cup of ketchup and the rest of seasoning.Then place all the fry chicken in the pot.

- Cover the pot and bring the mixture to a boil, about 10 minutes. Remove the lid and stir well,reduce the heat to low. Cover and simmer until the chicken is very tender and the gravy has reduced by half, about 40 minutes.

- Serve the chicken with rice and peas.

There are so many ways to cook brown stew chicken.
Enjoy this delicious dish...!

Printed in Great Britain
by Amazon

61895774R00022